ALBANIA TRAVEL GUIDE 2023

Beyond Borders: A Journey Through Albania's Rich Heritage

Travel Advisor

TABLE OF CONTENT

Chapter 1

Greetings from Albania

A brief history of Albania

Cultural and historical context

Chapter 2

Making Travel Plans for Albania

Albania's Best Time to Visit

Albanian visa requirements and entry procedures

Albanian Transportation Options

Albania's lodging options

Albania's financial planning and currency exchange

CHAPTER 3

Top Albanian Destinations

Tirana

Berat

Gjirokastra

Butrint

Saranda

Shkoder

National Park in Valbona Valley

Theft Park National

CHAPTER 4

Activities and Attractions

    Beaches and maritime pursuits

    trekking and hiking

    cultural encounters

    action sports

    places of interest and museums

CHAPTER 5

    food and beverage

        the traditional food of Albania

        Snacks and fast food

        Frequently sipped beverages

CHAPTER 6

    Useful Information

        Security advise and emergency numbers

        useful words and phrases

Conclusion

Chapter 1

Greetings from Albania

Welcome to Albania, a lovely nation with a rich history, fascinating culture, and a stunning natural setting in the center of the Balkans. You will find all the information you require in this guide to help you organize an enjoyable trip to Albania.

Every traveler may find something to enjoy in Albania, from the magnificent Albanian Alps to the clean beaches along the Adriatic and Ionian Seas. Albania won't let you down whether you're seeking excitement, relaxation, or cultural encounters.

You can learn about Albania's history, geography, and culture in this guide, along with useful advice on how to organize your travel arrangements, such as the need for a visa, available modes of transportation, and lodging alternatives. Additionally, you'll learn about some of Albania's greatest locations, points of interest, and activities, such as outdoor excursions, cultural encounters, and delectable cuisine and beverages.

Prepare to explore Albania's beauty and charm whether you're planning a solo trip or a family vacation. Start your exploration now!

A brief history of Albania

Albania is a little nation in southeast Europe, bordered to the northwest by Montenegro, to the northeast by Kosovo, to the east by North Macedonia, to the south by Greece, and to the west by the Adriatic and Ionian Seas. The ancient Illyrians, the Ottoman Empire, and the communist state that reigned until the early 1990s all had an impact on the country's rich history and culture. Albania is currently a well-liked travel destination because of its breathtaking natural beauty, rich history, and cultural heritage, mouthwatering cuisine, and friendly people. Albania offers activities for everyone, whether you want to visit historic sites, unwind on lovely beaches, or go climbing in the highlands.

Cultural and historical context

Albania has a lengthy, richly rooted history and cultural heritage. The Illyrians, Greeks, Romans, Byzantines, Ottomans, and Italians have all had an impact on the history, architecture, and culture of the nation.

Islam grew to be the preeminent faith in Albania during the almost 500-year Ottoman Empire's control. However, Albanians practice a distinctive synthesis of paganism, Christianity, and Islam.

Albania saw substantial political and socioeconomic transformations in the 20th century, including the installation of a communist administration that lasted from 1944 to 1992. Albania faced difficulties during the early 1990s transition to democracy and capitalism, including economic and political instability, but has since achieved tremendous progress in its growth.

Albania's numerous museums, archaeological sites, and historical landmarks, which draw tourists from all over the world, are examples of the country's cultural legacy today.

Chapter 2

Making Travel Plans for Albania

Albania, an undiscovered jewel of the Balkans, provides a special fusion of breathtaking landscapes, extensive history, and welcoming people. To get the most out of your trip, thorough planning is necessary for your trip to Albania. Here are a few crucial things to remember:

(1) Research and Itinerary: Begin by learning about Albania's major sights and locations. There are a variety of locations worth visiting, from the historic city of Butrint to the Albanian Riviera. Consider the time you have available and your interests when you plan your trip.

(2) Decide your intended stay in Albania. Set up enough time for each location depending on the number of locations you wish to see. It's important to keep in mind that Albania has a variety of attractions to offer, such as scenic beaches, ancient monuments, and hilly areas, so it's important to budget for a variety of experiences.

(3) Weather and Seasons: When organizing your vacation to Albania, it is essential to understand the local weather trends. The nation has a Mediterranean climate, which features hot summers and pleasant winters. The spring (April to June) and fall (September to October) shoulder seasons offer comfortable weather and fewer tourists.

(4) Local Customs & Etiquette: To ensure a courteous and enjoyable experience, familiarize yourself with the local customs and etiquette. Embracing Albanian culture will make your trip more memorable because Albanians are recognized for their friendliness and hospitality. To converse with the natives, it's beneficial to acquire a few fundamental Albanian words and phrases.

(5) Health and Safety: Travelers can feel secure when visiting Albania. However, it's wise to use the usual prudence by locking up your possessions and being watchful in public places. Before leaving for Albania, speak with your doctor about any recommended shots or prescriptions.

Albania's Best Time to Visit

Depending on your tastes and the kind of experience you're looking for, there is no one optimum time to visit Albania. Here are some crucial seasons to think about:

(1) Spring (April through June): The spring season brings pleasant weather and blossoming scenery. It's the perfect season for outdoor pursuits like mountain trekking and exploring historical places. This time of year, the landscape is unusually alive.

(2) Summer (July to August): If you enjoy the beach, summer is the ideal season to travel to Albania. During these months, the Riviera of Albania and other coastal regions are at their best. The sea is welcoming and warm, making it ideal for swimming and other aquatic activities.

(3) Autumn (September to October): The autumn months are ideal for exploring Albania's cultural treasures because they provide milder weather and fewer visitors. Landscapes are made more gorgeous by the fall leaves, especially in hilly areas.

(4) Winter in Albania is moderate along the coast but can be harsher in the mountains (November to March). This is the time of year to go if you like winter activities like skiing or wish to take part in customary Albanian winter celebrations.

Always check the forecast before your travel because, as we all know, the weather may be erratic.

Albanian visa requirements and entry procedures

Albania provides possibilities for visa-on-arrival or visa-free travel for lots of visitors. Here are some crucial details to remember about admission procedures and visa requirements:

(1) Visa-Free Entry: Individuals from the European Union (EU), the Schengen Area, the United States, Canada, Australia, and several other nations are not required to obtain a visa to enter Albania and remain there for up to 90 days inside a 180-day window.

(2) Visa-on-Arrival: At the airport or land border crossings, some nationalities—including India, China, Russia, and others—can receive a visa. For the most recent information, it is advised to visit the Albanian Ministry of Foreign Affairs official website.

Albanian Transportation Options

There are a variety of transportation choices available in Albania to accommodate various tastes and price ranges. The primary forms of transportation in Albania are as follows:

(1) Public Buses: In Albania, public buses are the most widely used and least expensive form of transportation both within and between cities. They connect important towns and popular tourist locations and provide wide coverage. Although the bus network is quite well-developed, schedules can occasionally be delayed. It is wise to look up the bus schedules in advance.

(2) Shared taxis and minibusses are both common modes of transportation for short distances inside cities or to

neighboring towns. Minibusses are also referred to as fourgons. They are shared taxis that travel along predetermined routes but do not adhere to a set schedule. Furgons are a practical means to get to places not served by normal buses and can be found at bus stations or designated stops.

(3) Train: Although Albania has a small train network, it can be a beautiful way to travel between some locations. The capital of Tirana is connected to Durrs, Shkodra, and Elbasan by train service. Despite being generally slower than buses, taking the train can be more enjoyable, especially when traveling through scenic areas.

(4) Renting a car allows you to explore Albania at your leisure and reach more rural locations. There are car rental agencies in large cities, tourist

destinations, and airports. You must be conversant with Albanian traffic laws and have a current international driver's license.

(5)Taxis: In cities and larger towns, taxis are easily accessible. It is advised to use authorized taxis with functional meters or to negotiate a fare in advance. Negotiating the fare is typical in tourist regions. Since Uber and other ride-hailing applications are not extensively used in Albania, employing local taxi services is the standard.

(6)   Ferries: If you want to go easily to coastal areas of Albania or surrounding islands like Saranda or Ksamil, use a ferry. Ferry services connect the mainland with several locations along the Albanian Riviera, and they may be a beautiful and pleasurable mode of transportation.

Albania's lodging options

Numerous lodging choices are available in Albania to accommodate various spending limits and tastes. Here are several well-liked options, which range from luxurious resorts to inexpensive hostels:

- Hotels: There are many hotels to choose from in major towns like Tirana, Durres, and Saranda, from opulent five-star hotels to boutique properties and reasonably priced lodgings. Hotels include services including Wi-Fi, breakfast, and private toilets. It's a good idea to make reservations in advance, especially during the busiest travel period.

- Bed and breakfasts and guesthouses: These accommodations offer a more personal and regional experience. These lodgings are typically managed by families and provide cozy rooms, warm hospitality, and home-cooked meals. They are an excellent method to get acquainted with Albanian culture.

- Vacation rentals: Thanks to the growth of websites like Airbnb, this has become a common choice in Albania. Vacation rentals, which range from flats to villas, provide the option of self-catering and a more comfortable setting. They can be found in both urban and rural settings.

- Camping is a wonderful way to see Albania outdoors because the country boasts stunning natural scenery. There are approved camping spots, especially in coastal and national parks. Before camping, make sure you are aware of the rules and amenities that are offered.

Albania's financial planning and currency exchange

Compared to many other European locations, Albania is renowned for providing travel experiences at reasonable prices. Here are some budgeting advice and information about currency exchange in Albania to help you maximize your trip and properly manage your costs:

- Currency: The Albanian Lek (ALL) is the country's legal tender. When you arrive, it's a good idea to exchange your money for Albanian Lek. Banks and authorized exchange offices are the most practical places to swap money. Cities and towns have a large number of ATMs, enabling you to get local cash as needed.

- Albania has a low cost of living when compared to other European nations.

In general, costs for meals, travel, and lodging are lower. However, be aware that popular tourist destinations might charge a little bit more. Prices are usually more reasonable in smaller towns and rural locations.

- Dining: If you choose to dine at neighborhood restaurants and traditional eateries, eating out in Albania can be reasonably priced. These restaurants provide delectable Albanian food at affordable pricing. Street food and local markets are fantastic places to find cheap meals if you're on a limited budget.

- Accommodations: As previously indicated, Albania offers a range of lodging choices to suit different budgets. While hotels and vacation rentals provide more comfort at higher price points, hostels, and guesthouses are great options for travelers on a budget. To find better discounts, think about staying in less popular places.

- Transportation: The cost of using Albania's public transportation is often low. Affordable fares are available for both short and long journeys on buses and minibusses. Although the network is small, train tickets are similarly fairly priced. Fuel and parking fees can make renting a car a little more pricey.

Activities and Sightseeing: Albania is home to many natural and cultural landmarks, many of which provide inexpensive or free admission. Visit historical sites, explore national parks, and engage in free or low-cost outdoor pursuits like swimming and hiking. Remember that certain guided excursions or attractions may require an entry fee.

Always carry some cash with you, especially if you're going somewhere distant where credit payments might not be readily accepted. However, hotels, eateries, and larger institutions typically accept credit and debit cards.

You may have a nice trip to Albania without going overboard if you prepare your budget and make wise decisions.

CHAPTER 3

Top Albanian Destinations

Welcome to Albania, a tiny but lovely nation in Southeast Europe renowned for its breathtaking natural beauty, extensive cultural legacy, and gracious hospitality. Albania is a nation with a lengthy and complicated past, which is represented in its buildings, food, and customs.

Albania has it all, whether you're searching for stunning mountain scenery, charming beach towns, or a bustling metropolis with a vivid history and culture. There is something for everyone in this interesting country, from the picturesque cobblestone alleyways of Berat and the lovely beaches of Saranda to the dynamic capital city of Tirana and the breathtaking natural wonders of the Albanian Alps.

We'll take you on a tour of Albania's greatest vacation spots in this guide, highlighting the top places to go, things to do, and experiences to have. So be ready to see Albania, one of Europe's most intriguing and developing countries!

Tirana

The vibrant and energetic city of Tirana, the capital of Albania, blends a long past with contemporary urban life. A variety of architectural types, including older Ottoman constructions and more recent Communist-era buildings, as well as hip cafes, restaurants, and bars can be found in Tirana.

Skanderbeg Square, named for the national hero who led the resistance against the Ottoman Empire, is one of Tirana's most well-known tourist destinations. The National History Museum, the Et'hem Bey Mosque, and the Clock Tower are all close by, making the area a center of activity.

The Bunk'Art museum, which is located in a sizable underground bunker constructed during the Communist era, is another must-see attraction in Tirana. The museum provides a fascinating look at life under Enver Hoxha's tyranny while also telling the tale of Albania's recent history.

In Tirana's thriving marketplaces, travelers may get anything from fresh produce to regional handicrafts. There are numerous restaurants and clubs in the city that include live music, DJs, and dancing, thus the nightlife there is also growing.

The neighboring Mount Dajti National Park offers an opportunity to see nature for those looking to get away from the city. It's a well-liked tourism destination for both residents and visitors since it has hiking routes, camping areas, and stunning vistas.

In general, Tirana is a city that has something to offer everyone, whether they want to learn about the past, experience the culture, or just take in the environment.

Berat

Known for its well-preserved Ottoman-era architecture and UNESCO World Heritage Site status, Berat is a medieval city in central Albania. The city is encircled by hills and mountains and is located on the banks of the Osum River.

Due to the numerous windows on the whitewashed homes that ascend the hillside of the old town, Berat is frequently referred to as the "City of a Thousand Windows". With influences from the Illyrian, Roman, Byzantine, Ottoman, and contemporary Albanian cultures, the city has a rich cultural legacy.

The historic fortress, which is one of Berat's most notable attractions, is situated on a hill above the city. Visitors can tour the ruins of a medieval castle, three ancient mosques, and an Orthodox church from the fourteenth century inside the citadel. A 15th-century mosque, various museums, and winding lanes lined with Ottoman-era homes can be found in Mangalem, the lower town of Berat.

The food of Berat is also well-known, particularly the regional wines and classic dishes such as burek (savory pastries filled with cheese, meat, or vegetables) and Kosi (baked lamb with yogurt).

Gjirokastra

One of the most stunning cities in Albania is Gjirokastra, which is also a UNESCO World Heritage Site. It is renowned for its exquisite Ottoman-era architecture and is occasionally referred to as the "city of stone" because of the numerous stone residences that line its winding, narrow lanes.

The Gjirokastra Castle, which is perched on a hilltop and offers a view of the city, is one of the most recognizable structures in this region. The fortress was the scene of numerous conflicts throughout history and dates to the 12th century.

The Skenduli House, a beautifully preserved Ottoman-era home that has been turned into a museum, the Ethnographic Museum, which exhibits daily life among Albanians in the 19th and 20th centuries, and the Zekate House, another Ottoman-era home that has been turned into a museum, are among the other noteworthy attractions in Gjirokastra.

The traditional food of Gjirokastra is also well-known. Dishes like wifi (meatballs made with rice and herbs), me mish (a stew of meat and vegetables), and flija (a stacked pancake made with cornmeal and eaten with cheese) are just a few examples.

Gjirokastra is surrounded by stunning natural landscapes, notably the Drino Valley and the Vjosa River, in addition to its cultural and historical landmarks. Outdoor enthusiasts who want to go hiking, biking, and kayaking will love it there.

Butrint

Ancient Butrint can be found in southern Albania, close to the Greek border. It has been recognized as a UNESCO World Heritage Site and is one of the most significant archaeological sites in the nation. The ancient Greeks built the city of Butrint in the seventh century BC, and the Romans, Byzantines, and Venetians all afterward inhabited there. The city was a significant hub for trade and culture in the area and the structures and fortifications that now stand as proof of its former wealth and prosperity.

The ruins of the old theater, the agora, the basilica, and the baptistery are just a few of the many sights that visitors to Butrint can explore. The spectacular defensive walls of the city, which were constructed during the Byzantine era, are another well-liked tourist attraction.

Butrint is surrounded by lush forests and wetlands that are home to a wide range of plant and animal species, making it part of a stunning natural setting. Nature lovers and outdoor enthusiasts frequently travel to the Butrint National Park, which is home to the historic city and the natural landscapes around it.

Overall, Butrint is a must-visit location for anybody visiting Albania since it provides visitors with a distinctive fusion of history, culture, and natural beauty.

Saranda

Albania's southern region is home to the lovely beach city of Saranda. Due to its beautiful beaches, clean waters, and mild Mediterranean environment, it is a well-liked vacation spot. Saranda is a great location for those interested in learning about the nation's past because of its illustrious history and cultural heritage.

The historic city of Butrint, a UNESCO World Heritage Site that dates back to the 7th century BC, is among the most well-liked sights in Saranda. Visitors can visit the ancient city's ruins, which include

Byzantine churches, a Roman forum, and Venetian towers.

Along with other stunning beaches, Saranda is also home to the well-known Mirror Beach and Ksamil Beach. These beaches are renowned for their crystal-clear seas and fine, white sand, making them the ideal locations for sunbathing and relaxation.

Saranda is renowned for its mouthwatering cuisine and lively nightlife in addition to its natural beauty. One of the city's numerous eateries and cafes serves up fresh seafood and traditional Albanian fare, and visitors may dance the night away at one of its vibrant nightclubs.

Saranda has something to offer everyone, whether they are interested in history, or culture, or just want to unwind on the beach.

Shkoder

Shkoder is a city in northwest Albania that is close to the Montenegrin border. It is one of Albania's oldest and most historic cities and offers visitors a distinctive fusion of natural beauty, culture, and history. The city is encircled by the Albanian Alps and is located close to the lovely Lake Skadar.

The following are some of the top attractions in Shkoder:

- Located on a hilltop with a view of the city and Lake Skadar is the old castle known as Rozafa Castle.
- The Marubi National Museum of Photography is home to a significant collection of old photographs and photographic-related objects.
- Shkoder Cathedral: A stunning cathedral that was first constructed in the 1800s and is situated in the heart of the city.

- The largest lake in the Balkans, Lake Skadar, is renowned for its breathtaking natural beauty and distinct ecosystem.
- Mes Bridge: A historic bridge from the Ottoman Empire that is situated in the heart of the city.
- Buna River: a well-liked location for trekking, fishing, and kayaking.
- Taraboshi Mountain: A stunning mountain range that is easily accessible from the city and well-liked by outdoor enthusiasts.

Along with these sights, Shkoder is renowned for its vibrant atmosphere and active nightlife. The city is renowned for its delectable cuisine, which combines Balkan and Mediterranean flavors. Fries, a baked dish with peppers, tomatoes, and cheese, and tav Kosi, a filling dish with lamb, rice, and yogurt, are a couple of the must-try foods in Shkoder.

Overall, Shkoder is an excellent choice for tourists who want to take in Albania's rich history and natural beauty as well as the city's active culture and nightlife.

National Park in Valbona Valley

In the northern region of Albania, close to the borders with Montenegro and Kosovo, sits Valbona Valley National Park. It is famous for its breathtaking mountain scenery, which includes the Valbona River, Valbona Valley, and the Albanian Alps. It has a surface area of about 8,000 hectares.

The paths and valleys of Valbona Valley National Park are ideal for hiking, mountain biking, and horseback riding. Along with numerous rare plant species, the park is also home to a variety of fauna, including bears, wolves, and lynx.

The Valbona to Theth trek, which takes 6 to 8 hours to complete and offers breathtaking views of the Valbona Valley and surrounding mountains, is one of the most well-liked hiking routes in the park. When the weather is pleasant and the track is well-maintained, June to September are the optimum months to tackle the trail.

The surrounding settlements of Valbona and Theth are home to a large number of guesthouses and lodges that are open to park visitors. These inns are a wonderful way to get a feel for the culture and way of life of the area because they provide cozy lodging and authentic Albanian cuisine.

Theft Park National

In the northern region of the country, in the Albanian Alps, is the stunning natural reserve known as Theth National Park. It is named after the charming village of Theth, which is situated inside the park and spans a surface area of 2,630 hectares. The park is renowned for its spectacular mountain scenery, conventional Albanian architecture, and hiking paths that provide breathtaking views of the neighboring peaks and valleys.

The Grunas Waterfall, a 30-meter-high waterfall encircled by thick greenery, is one of the park's principal attractions. Hikers can take a beautiful walk through the park's forests and meadows to get to the waterfall.

The Blue Eye, a natural spring with brilliant blue water, is another well-liked destination in Theth National Park. Swim in the refreshing spring water or unwind under the adjacent trees' shade.

There are numerous hiking paths available in Theth National Park for hikers of different skill levels. The Valbona to Theth Trail, which takes hikers through the Albanian Alps and provides breathtaking views of the surrounding mountains, and the Radohima Peak Trail, a strenuous climb that leads to Radohima Peak's peak, are two of the most well-known trails.

Theth National Park is a must-visit location for outdoor enthusiasts, hikers, and anybody else interested in taking in the breathtaking splendor of the Albanian Alps.

CHAPTER 4

Activities and Attractions

Welcome to our section on attractions and activities in Albania. Travelers may enjoy a variety of experiences in Albania, from seeing medieval towns and ancient ruins to hiking through breathtaking national parks and relaxing on gorgeous beaches. This section will walk you through Albania's must-see sights and activities and provide you with all the details you need to make the most of your trip. So get ready to experience Albania's greatest features!

Beaches and maritime pursuits

Beach enthusiasts frequently travel to Albania because of its beautiful Adriatic and Ionian Sea coastlines. Albania has some of the top beaches in the world:

- Dhrmi Beach: This beach, which is on the southern coast, is renowned for its pristine seas and fine white sand.
- Ksamil Beach: Ksamil Beach, which is located close to the southern border with Greece, is known for its turquoise waters and several small islands.
- Gjipe Beach is a secret paradise nestled in a cove between two cliffs and is only reachable by boat or a strenuous climb.
- Jale Beach: Jale Beach, close to the village of Himara, is renowned for its breathtaking views and crystal-clear waters.

Albania offers a variety of coastal activities in addition to beaches, including swimming, snorkeling, and diving.

Mountain hiking, touring historic sites and ruins, and taking in the local cuisine and culture are some of the other well-liked things to do in Albania.

trekking and hiking

Outdoor enthusiasts, especially hikers, and trekkers, will find Albania to be a paradise. The nation is a great place to go on an adventure because it has so many national parks, mountain ranges, and hiking trails.
The Albanian Alps, Mount Tomorr, the Valbona Valley National Park, and Theth National Park are some of the most well-liked places to do hiking and trekking in Albania.
Hikers and trekkers can take in the breathtaking scenery, immaculate lakes, lush forests, and traditional communities in

these regions. The Peaks of the Balkans Trail, the Komani Lake Trail, and the Llogara Pass Trail are a few of Albania's most well-known hiking routes.

Every outdoor enthusiast, regardless of experience level, may find something to enjoy in Albania.

cultural encounters

With influences from the ancient Illyrians, the Greeks, the Romans, and the Ottomans, Albania is a nation rich in history and culture. Visitors visiting Albania have a range of opportunities to explore the distinctive cultural legacy of the nation, including:

- Attending festivals and celebrations: Because Albanians are recognized for their joie de vivre, the nation holds several exciting events all year long, such as the Kala Festival in Dhrmi, the Gjirokastra National Folklore Festival, and the Tirana International Film Festival.

- Discovering traditional villages: Theth and Valbona are just two of the attractive traditional villages in Albania where tourists may get a taste of the country's past.
- Trying local cuisine and beverages: Visitors can try traditional foods like frges, tav kosi, and byrek as well as regional wines and raki. Albanian cuisine is a delightful blend of Mediterranean and Balkan flavors.
- Taking in traditional performances: Visitors to Albania can take in traditional performances like the Iso-Polyphony, a style of polyphonic singing that has been designated as a UNESCO intangible cultural property.

Every visitor may find something to enjoy in Albania, whether they are into music, gastronomy, or history.

action sports

Albania is a well-liked vacation spot for thrill enthusiasts because it provides a variety of adventure activities. The country's untamed terrain and vast coastline offer chances for a wide range of sports, including:

- With Class II to IV rapids, the Vjosa River is one of the most well-liked rafting locations in Albania.
- Canyoning: The Osumi Canyon is a well-liked location for canyoning, with a variety of courses to suit all skill levels.
- Paragliding: Popular locations for paragliding in Albania include the coastal town of Vlora and the Albanian Alps.
- Rock climbing: The Karaburun Peninsula and the Valbona Valley National Park both provide good rock climbing options.

- Off-roading: There are several opportunities for off-roading in the Albanian countryside, particularly in the Sharr and Tomorr Mountains.
- Skiing is possible in the Albanian Alps, with Valbona Valley National Park being the most well-liked location.
- Skydiving: Tandem jumps are an option for beginners when skydiving in Tirana.

Just a few of the adventure sports Albania offers are listed above. The country is a great choice for travelers looking for adventure due to its diverse terrain and stunning scenery.

places of interest and museums

Albania has a lengthy and intriguing history, and the nation is home to several monuments and museums that shed light on that history. The most prominent ones are as follows:

- The history of Albania, from ancient times to the present, is the focus of the National Historical Museum in Tirana.
- The Tirana Ethnographic Museum features displays of clothes, household objects, and other artifacts to illustrate traditional Albanian life and culture.
- The pottery, jewelry, and statues in the Archaeological Museum of Durres are examples of relics from the historic city of Dyrrachium, which is located in the seaside city of Durres.
- Butrint National Park - This park's natural beauty is complemented by the ruins of a UNESCO World Heritage Site, which comprise

structures from the ancient civilizations of the Greeks, Romans, and Byzantines.

- The Skanderbeg Museum in Kruja is devoted to Albania's national hero Skanderbeg and features displays about both his life and the history of the nation at the time.
- Tirana's Museum of Albanian Philately houses a large collection of Albanian stamps, many of which are rare and expensive.
- Apollonia Archaeological Park - This park, which is close to the town of Fier, has the remains of a former Greek city, including a theater, a temple, and other buildings.

These are only a few of Albania's numerous historical sites and museums. Through these encounters, tourists may delve into the interesting past of the nation and learn more about its culture and traditions.

CHAPTER 5

food and beverage

Albanian food combines Mediterranean and Balkan influences and places a big focus on using fresh, regional ingredients. Albanian cuisine is sure to gratify any food lover with its hearty meat dishes and delicious seafood. Along with its distinctive cuisine, Albania has a long history of winemaking, with numerous renowned wineries spread around the nation. So be ready to revel in Albania's delectable cuisine and beverages when you arrive.

the traditional food of Albania

Balkan, Mediterranean, and Ottoman influences are all present in Albanian cuisine. The food has a robust flavor and is renowned for using a lot of herbs and spices. Typically, fresh, regional ingredients like vegetables, meat, fish, and dairy products are used to prepare Albanian meals.

Popular Albanian dishes include the following:

- Tave Kosi: A filling dish of rice and lamb baked with yogurt and eggs and seasoned with herbs and garlic.
- A pastry stuffed with cheese, spinach, or meat is called a byrek.
- A hot stew cooked with peppers, tomatoes, and cheese is called a frage.
- A meatball consisting of ground lamb or beef and flavored with parsley, onions, and garlic is known as a qofte.
- A sweet pastry formed from layers of phyllo dough, honey, and almonds is called baklava.
- A cool, hydrating soup made with yogurt, cucumber, garlic, and dill is called tarator.
- Tullumba: A sweet pastry made of fried dough and syrup.

Albania is also well-known for its top-notch wine, which is made in the southern part of the nation. Shesh I Zi, Kallmet, and Merlot are popular types.

Overall, Albanian food offers a varied and savory eating experience that captures the rich history and culture of the nation.

Snacks and fast food

Albanian street cuisine is a vital component of the nation's culinary landscape and a must-try experience. Here are some of Albania's most well-liked snacks and street food:

- A delicious pastry stuffed with cheese, meat, or vegetables is called a byrek.
- Qofte is seasoned beef, lamb, or chicken meatballs.
- Grilled meat skewers known as kebabs are often produced from lamb or chicken.
- A pie-like dish composed of veggies, cheese, and meat is called a "piete."

- Grilled lamb or goat intestines wrapped in pita bread are known as kokorec.
- Lamb, rice, and yogurt are combined to make the baked meal tav kosi.
- Lakror is a thin flatbread stuffed with meat, cheese, or vegetables and baked.
- Flija is a layered pastry with yogurt and honey that is created from thin crepes.

All around Albania, you may get these street dishes and snacks at little stores or food carts in local markets and town squares. They are frequently served with several sauces and dips, such as tarator (a yogurt and cucumber dip), ajvar (a red pepper and eggplant spread), and chili sauce.

Frequently sipped beverages

Albania has a vibrant gastronomic tradition that also permeates its libations. Several well-liked non-alcoholic beverages are:

- Boza is a fermented beverage that is sweet, thick, and prepared from wheat, corn, or barley.
- Joghurt is a cool yogurt beverage that is frequently flavored with mint or cucumber.
- Soda: There are many different carbonated beverages and soft drinks available in Albania.
- Coffee is a popular beverage among Albanians, and coffee culture is a significant aspect of daily life. The most popular coffee is Turkish-style.

Regarding alcoholic beverages, there is a variety to choose from:

- Raki is a potent spirit frequently used as an aperitif or digestif that is prepared from grapes or other fruits.

- Beer: Popular Albanian beer brands include Birra Tirana, Korça, and Peja.
- Wine - There are numerous regional varietals to sample, and Albania has a long history of wine production.
- Vermouth - Made from regional herbs and botanicals, Sknderbeu Vermouth is the brand of vermouth that Albania makes.
- In the winter, rakomelo, a traditional Albanian liqueur prepared from raki and honey, is frequently served heatedly.

CHAPTER 6

Useful Information

Welcome to our section of our travel guide to Albania devoted to practical information! You can find all the information you require here to prepare for your trip to Albania. We have you covered on everything from visa requirements to money exchange, safety advice, and more. To get you ready for a delightful and hassle-free experience in Albania, let's get started now.

Security advise and emergency numbers

Keep in mind the following safety advice and emergency numbers when traveling in Albania:

- Keep an eye on your stuff at all times and be on the lookout for pickpockets, especially in crowded places like marketplaces, buses, and tourist destinations.

- Avoid unmarked taxis and unreliable drivers by using licensed taxis or ride-sharing applications for transportation.
- Avoid going alone at night or in remote locations.
- Stick to authorized routes and observe municipal ordinances for safety whether hiking or trekking.
- When swimming in the sea, use caution because strong currents and undertows can be harmful.
- Call 112 for police, fire, or medical assistance in an emergency.
- Visit a hospital or clinic in a large city like Tirana, Durres, or Vlore for non-emergency medical care.
- Having travel insurance that provides coverage for theft, evacuation, and medical situations is an excellent idea.

You can travel to Albania safely and successfully if you bear these suggestions in mind.

useful words and phrases

Yes, the following words and phrases in Albanian are helpful:

- Hello: Përshëndetje
- Goodbye: Mirupafshim
- Yes: Po
- No: Jo
- Please: Ju lutem
- Thank you: Faleminderit
- Excuse me: Më falni
- Sorry: Më falni
- How much does it cost?: Sa kushton kjo?
- Where is the bathroom?: Ku është banjoja?
- I don't speak Albanian: Nuk flas shqip

- Do you speak English?: Flisni anglisht?
- Help!: Ndihmë!
- Police: Policia
- Hospital: Spitali
- Pharmacy: Farmacia

Although English is widely used in larger towns and tourist regions in Albania, Albanian is the country's official language. To make communication smoother, it is always beneficial to know a few fundamental Albanian terms.

Conclusion

I sincerely hope that my travel guide has been educational and useful to you as you plan your vacation to Albania. Albania is a lovely nation with a fascinating past, vibrant culture, and breathtaking natural scenery. There is something for every kind of traveler in Albania, from the ancient cities of Tirana and Berat to the breathtaking beaches of Saranda and the national parks of Valbona and Theth.

Make sure to sample traditional Albanian food, immerse yourself in the community, and take part in the many events and attractions Albania has to offer. Always remember to take precautions, respect other cultures, and take pleasure in your trips.

Made in United States
Troutdale, OR
08/16/2023

12122595R10035